# Companions
## along the way

Poems from 1998 to 2020

by
Deanna Klein Shapiro

Burlington
Vermont

Cover and interior art by Deanna Klein Shapiro
facebook.com/deannakleinshapiro
Prepress design and layout: Linda Tyler

Copyright ©2021 by Deanna Klein Shapiro
All rights reserved. No part of this publication may be reproduced, distributed, or transmitted in any form or by any means, including photocopying, recording, or other electronic or mechanical methods, without the prior written permission of the publisher, except in the case of brief quotations embodied in critical reviews and certain other noncommercial uses permitted by copyright law.

ISBN: 978-1-7923-6273-6
Library of Congress Control Number: 2021904804

Onion River Press
191 Bank Street
Burlington, VT  05401

For Holly Shapiro, Emily Shapiro,
Sofia Herfter and Gabriela Herfter

*To pay attention, this is our endless and proper work.*
                                       Mary Oliver

Also by Deanna Klein Shapiro

*Conversations at the Nursing Home: A Mother, A Daughter and Alzheimer's*

*The Place You Live In: A Multigenerational Immigrant Story*

*On the Road with Lewis and Clark and Other Considerations: A Diary* (chapbook)

## Table of Contents

| | |
|---|---|
| Acknowledgements | viii |
| Preface | ix |
| **SPIRIT AND NATURE** | |
| When I Hang Out the Wash | 15 |
| Maiden with Bowl Statue | 16 |
| Woman of Spirit I | 17 |
| Woman of Spirit II | 18 |
| Woman of Spirit III | 19 |
| The History of My Breath | 20 |
| Seven Stanzas on Stillness at the Time of the Pandemic | 21 |
| Inner Work | 22 |
| Unity | 23 |
| The Old Oak Tree | 24 |
| Taking Action | 25 |
| Night | 26 |
| Illusions | 27 |
| Holocaust Remembrance Day | 28 |
| Ritual | 29 |
| Everything in Place | 30 |
| Awareness | 31 |
| Miracles | 32 |
| Ordinary Day | 33 |
| Shellhouse Mountain | 34 |
| Hardy Pleasures | 35 |
| Late September Walk | 37 |
| Behold | 38 |
| Mothers | 39 |
| Ravens | 40 |
| Crone | 41 |
| The Sounds of Water | 42 |
| Say Have You Seen the Sumac? | 43 |
| Spring Walk | 44 |
| Mutual Refreshment | 45 |
| On My Knees | 46 |
| T'ai Chi with Gray Catbird | 47 |
| Words in the Time of the Pandemic | 48 |

## PEOPLE AND PLACES

| | |
|---|---|
| There You Were | 55 |
| You Do What You Gotta Do | 56 |
| Prayer Poem for Alan | 57 |
| Portraits | 58 |
| Heritage | 60 |
| Mrs. Samuels | 62 |
| Companions | 63 |
| Exemplary Lives | 65 |
| Wait Awhile | 66 |
| Displaced | 67 |
| Visit with Carolyn | 69 |
| At the Memory Unit | 70 |
| Telling Stories | 71 |
| Coming up on 91 | 72 |
| In the Moment | 73 |
| You Took Us In | 75 |
| History Lesson | 76 |
| Kindergarten Teachers | 77 |
| Waiting for a Procedure | 78 |
| Mobile | 79 |
| Northern Latitudes | 81 |
| In the Champlain Valley | 82 |
| Architecture for the Soul | 83 |
| Reflections on Lake Champlain | 84 |
| Island Mentality | 86 |
| Island Life | 87 |
| On Top of Whiteface Mountain | 88 |
| Open Mic at Carol's Hungry Mind Café | 89 |
| At the Annual Town Meeting in Ferrisburgh, Vermont | 90 |
| At the Yarn Shop | 91 |
| At Harry's Bar in Gainesville, Florida on New Year's Eve | 92 |
| Birding on the Gulf Coast | 93 |
| Morning Walk on the Gulf Coast | 94 |
| The Gulf Coast in Winter | 95 |
| How to Ride the New York City Subway | 96 |
| New York City Travel | 98 |
| Tiny Tales from Public School 26 | 99 |

## ARTISTS AND WRITERS

| | |
|---|---|
| The Red Studio | 109 |
| A Question for Milton Avery | 110 |
| On Encountering Henry Moore's Sculpture | 111 |
| Paul Klee's Fantasmagoria | 112 |
| The Gentle Painter | 113 |
| Reading Gabriele Munter | 114 |
| Chagall's Dalliance | 115 |
| My Dearest Edouard Vuillard | 116 |
| Charles Burchfield's Salem | 117 |
| About Franz Kline's Black and White No. 2 | 118 |
| My Dinner in Finland | 119 |
| Children of the Sun | 120 |
| Jean Dubuffet's Transgressions | 121 |
| Inuit Artists of Hudson Bay | 122 |
| In Emily Carr's Canadian Forests | 123 |
| Melancholy | 124 |
| Tulip | 125 |
| Swimming in Abstractions | 126 |
| Tulips and Irises | 127 |
| Van Gogh Took His Reed Pen | 128 |
| Zen Painting: Mu Chi'i's Persimmons | 129 |
| Pic Island, Lake Superior | 130 |
| Charles Augustus Smith | 131 |
| Exhalation | 132 |
| Mentor | 134 |
| My Childhood Poet | 136 |
| An Unknown Woman | 137 |
| Journal of a Solitude | 138 |
| For Stevie Smith | 140 |
| Emily and Me | 142 |

## Acknowledgements

Thank you, David Weinstock and the Otter Creek Poets, for twenty-two years of valuable feedback. Thank you, Poetry Pod of the Suncoast Writers Guild, for nurturing my poetry. Thank you, Poetry Society of Vermont, for helping to sharpen my poetry and editing skills. Thank you, Alice Leventhal, for friendship and thorough critiques. Thank you, Roma Mortensen, for friendship and creative suggestions. Thank you to my husband, Charlie, for his sacrifices and encouragement. Thank you, Holly Shapiro Herfter and Emily Shapiro Belth, for endless support and encouragement. Thank you, Linda Tyler, for your knowledge of layout and design and your congenial, upbeat attitude. Thank you, Rachel Fisher, of Onion River Press, for your expertise and guidance. Thank you, Dave Sullivan, for patient and generous technical support. Thank you to all the people and places that have enriched my life, and have been companions along the way.

Grateful acknowledgement is made to the following publications in which poems in this volume were first published, sometimes in a slightly different form.

*The Mountain Troubadour*: Illusion, Ritual, On Encountering Henry Moore's Sculpture, Maiden with Bowl Statue, The Old Oak Tree
*Addison Independent*: Everything in Place
*Tapestries*: Shellhouse Mountain
*Penwood Review*: There You Were, Woman of Spirit I, Emily and Me: A Sestina
*Blueline*: When I Hang Out the Wash
*The Vital Force*: Unity, Seven Stanzas on Stillness in the Time of the Pandemic
*ZigZagLitMag*: Tulip
*Burlington Art Journal*: On Encountering Henry Moore's Sculpture

## Preface

Many years ago, I was sitting at my desk in my bedroom, looking out on a clump of birch trees and the winter sun setting behind them. I was paying bills. As I paid the bill for the *Save the Children* foundation those words, *Save the Children*, jumped out at me from the payment stub in a startling way. At the time, I was raising two daughters and had been a kindergarten teacher and school psychologist in elementary schools. So children were already a strong part of my life.

It was a heart-filled, breathtaking moment. But I didn't know what to do about that command. And I didn't know I would be called upon to write poetry.

For many years, I tried to find information about the lives of generations that came before me—the generations whose shoulders I stand on.

So I see the poems in this book, in previous books, and books still to come, as gifts to the generations that come after me. These poems embody a narrative, a diary, from one ancestral point of view—a dive into one's history. This, then, is my way of *Saving the Children* in my family—fulfilling that earlier command—by making it easier for them to know their roots; that is, if they have a thirst for family knowledge, as I did.

However, it is my hope that readers of this book, of any generation, will feel the experiences that I felt and put into writing.

This book is divided into three sections: Spirit and Nature, People and Places, and Artists and Writers. All the poems represent subjects that caught my attention, my heart, and became my companions along the way.

Deanna Klein Shapiro
Shellhouse Mountain Farm
January, 2021

# SPIRIT AND NATURE

## When I Hang Out the Wash

In the other house
we had a European clothesline,
rope woven between wooden T-posts
anchored in the ground.
*I want one of those,* I told my husband
on a French holiday.
It looked rugged and honest.

Now we have a portable one
out on the porch, Australian design,
bought online, the rope threaded
between metal stanchions
like a music staff waiting for a composer.

I grasp three clothespins from the denim bag.
Nine geese honk over Lake Champlain.
I pick a damp sock, underpants, and washcloth
from the basket. Their moisture cools my skin.
I hang each one, then take three more.
My tempo slows.
Clouds curl in on themselves
over navy Adirondack peaks.
Clothespins stand like wooden notes,
line by orderly line, obediently holding clothes,
ready to greet wind and sun.
A chickadee sings on top of the porch wall.
Tomatoes in the garden hang ripe and ready.
And here am I,
lingering like a whole note in a rhapsody.

**Maiden with Bowl Statue**

When I first saw her
at Green Valley Nursery
I instantly knew
she was mine.

Now humble and silent
she stands in my Japanese garden
sweetly draped in her robe—
shawl collar, sash with a bow
in back—
hair upswept in a bun,
head slightly bent,
quiet downward gaze.
She holds a bowl in her arms.
*Wash your weary bones here,*
she says.

Divine lady—friend
of the bee balm
and turnip,
the box turtle,
barn swallow,
and bobcat,

kind maiden—I know you—
you who live in the wind currents
and the tide.
I will be with you
where bamboo sways
and the water is clear.

**Woman of Spirit I**

Mrs. Nolt pulled blueberry muffins
from the oven—humming, unhurried,
preparing our big farm breakfast,
sang hymns in her kitchen
canning red ripe tomatoes,
conversed with a Mennonite neighbor
on her porch, let down her braided
strawberry blonde hair in the night.
She stared out at the world
through thick, rimless glasses—
told her grandchildren,
*God gave us weaknesses and this is mine.*

When she gestured with her hand,
up from her belly,
signaling strength she drew from within—
when her daughter, for example,
called about a crisis—
something substantial stirred within me,
recalled a spirit of long ago,
set a flower germinating
through cracked and arid soil.

## Woman of Spirit II

Hazel Archer, photographer,
captured people in moments of truth.
Disabled by polio, she was carried
where crutches and wheelchair couldn't take her.
Compassionate wrinkles framed her dark eyes.

I met her in Santa Fe at one of her lectures
on her *high humanitarians*—
Buckminster Fuller, Maria Montessori,
Joseph Goldsmith.

The words of this spider woman,
this muse—this grandmother—
her words—they prodded me.
*Tune in, girl. Tune in! Get rid of the static.*
*Hear the clear voice of Heaven.*

Hazel Archer, she compelled me
to grasp the silken strands of my life,
endorse their colors,
and weave them deftly
into a multi-colored tapestry.

**Woman of Spirit III**

Eula Bruce, owner of the tribal arts shop
where we stopped to buy a Navajo rug,
bought her crafts at local Indian reservations,
one of the few white women welcomed
by the Navajo, Hopi and Zuni.

She, a stranger we encountered in the desert,
who engaged us in conversation,
must have noticed something unspoken
beneath my words, a certain prayerful place
I didn't know was showing.

She gave me her worn copy of Krishnamurti,
blessing me like an Indian mother.

**The History of My Breath**

Oh, Breath, how little I knew you
in my youth. You were soft and shallow—
I, afraid to embrace you—
feelings frozen in strict submission
to a father's demands.

I inhaled anxiety from birth,
an empath absorbing my mother's memory
of her mother's early death—
when she was only two.

Relaxation teachers introduced me to you,
taught me to breathe into body parts—
from my toes to the crown of my head.
My Lamaze teacher taught me
to pant through childbirth contractions.

Meditation teachers taught me
to focus on you—
in-breath, out-breath,
the pause between.

Oh, Breath, rescue me from
mundane concerns, rooted impediments,
outlying obstacles,

take me deep
where underground waters flow.

**Seven Stanzas on Stillness at the Time of the Pandemic**

They say people sheltering in place
are experiencing enforced stillness.
Stillness—reflection—cannot be forced.
Still it's a good time to give stillness its due

because stillness is like a giving tree
offering gifts
of serenity,
insights, safety.

Stillness is like a summer breeze
offering an opening
to follow our breath—inhaling—exhaling,
time to be our breath.

Stillness is like clear water
offering a channel
to our creativity,
our intuition, our essence.

Stillness is like a loving friend
offering a way
to acknowledge feelings,
accept what is, nourish our spirit.

Stillness is like a walk down a path
offering time
to enter into mystery and meaning,
the eternal.

Stillness is like an orchestra's harmony
offering an attitude
that softens hearts, eradicates judgment,
eliminates separateness.

It's a good time to give stillness its due.

**Inner Work**

I have listened deeply.

I have opened myself to past suffering and pain.
I have cleared out cobwebs of resentment.
I have handled shame.
I have addressed jealousies.
I have embraced lifelong anxiety.
I have let go of resistance to what is.
I have wrapped my inner child in a blanket of love.

I have softened my heart.
I have nourished my spirit.
I have learned how to quiet my mind.
I have worked with forgiveness.
I have opened space for presence.
I have practiced lovingkindness and gratitude.
I have prayed always.

I feel rooted like the old oak tree in my driveway.

Yet I am only as good as my awareness in each moment.

**Unity**

I am out here on the porch
doing T'ai Chi Chih,
facing Shellhouse Mountain,
a cathedral of craggy rocks and pines.

My body is easy
like the brown speckled snake
sunning against the house,
head cocked at an angle.

I am energized like the hummingbird
drinking nectar from the bee balm,
the Monarch butterfly fluttering among the phlox,
the grosbeaks flying straight from tree to feeder,

carried on the radiant morning highway.

## The Old Oak Tree

In folk art embellished birds sit in a tree
on outstretched branches—
set at intervals like ornaments—
a decorative pattern.

I observed crows sitting that way
the other day in the towering oak
on my driveway—
one of three we love
that drew us to the property.

This colossal giant who stands bravely
in rain, snow, and wind,
lost branches in the last ice storm.
It shades the pasture,
shelters animals,
makes acorns for squirrels,
seeds for new growth.

Dressed in rugged bark
like the wrinkled skin of wise elders,
its rooted trunk stands steadfast
like a stately cathedral.
Its brawny branches brush the sky,
reach for the heavens,
accepting, giving—
teaching enlightenment.

**Taking Action**

Rabbi Abraham Joshua Heschel said:
*Prayer is no substitute for action.*
He prayed with his feet, walking in Selma
with Martin Luther King.
Judaism isn't big on monasteries or monks.
Its aim is *tikkun olam*, repair of the world.

But I am monkish. I am an artist.
How can art feed the hungry,
heal the oppressed?

Finally an answer:
I pray with my brush and pen—
painting and writing for the soul,
for the spirit to soar.
This is my assignment—paint and write—
keep your own fire burning.

**Night**

To be surrounded by the sky at night,
to be enveloped in the dark expanse,
as purple clouds sail by and do enhance,
the universe, its mystery and its might,
where mountains deep reflect the sparkling light,
of ordered stars imbedded in their dance,
and round moon smiles so brightly at your glance,
through blackened trees reached up to grandest height.

A tiny soul standing out there alone,
may comfort take in facing the unknown,
opening heart and mind to nature's call,
breathing deeply the night's protective shawl,
where God projects his loving, joyful force,
for all who choose to know His Divine source.

**Illusions**

It is April. It has rained all day,
sometimes hard with meaning,
washing everything frantically,
its onslaught pounding the roof,
accompanying me as I work
inside my cocoon.

Now, at dusk, the sky,
still overcast across Lake Champlain,
presses down on the Adirondacks—
mist hovering after the rain—
shrouding it in opaque shades of gray—
a soft backdrop for the leafless line
of murky trees bordering the lake,
slender branches reaching up,
firm in their praise of the heavens.

**Holocaust Remembrance Day**

The sun glistens on pristine snow.
The air is tart and crisp.
Blue skies cheer the day.
Chickadees bounce
from copper cypress
to Harry Lauder walking stick
to mountain ash.

I hear the frigid wind roaring.
Tree trunks list left, then right,
their bare branches straining.
It pushes hard against me
when I fill the bird feeders.

Its penetrating chill lingers
in my body on the way
to the planning meeting for Yom HaShoah
as I focus on the numbing reality
of this remembrance
which we always carry with us.

**Ritual**

There was something about
cooking carrots for our friends' dinner—
brightly colored buttons
in a coat of avocado oil,
submerged in bubbling orange juice,
speckled with grated ginger,
the variegated color of friendship
mounded to the brim
of a ten-inch pot.

There was something about
the muffled boiling
under the pot lid—
like the whispers of lovers,
the fluttering of hummingbirds,
a Debussy Prelude.

**Everything in Place**

I am learning to make friends with dying,
an unspoken topic where I come from.
They say it's as easy as waves
breaching the shore, as graceful
as a porpoise surfacing, arcing,
as light as a sunny day watching him—
sand squishing through your toes.

The white begonia,
the centerpiece from Sunday's party,
poses on the desk in my sitting room,
the pot still wrapped in purple foil,
no plate under it yet to collect water.
The morning is gray; the day is cold.
I sit in my recliner, warmed
by my striped wool blanket
and gas fireplace glowing in the corner.
A bookcase of friends covers one wall—
everything the way I always imagined it.
A basket of books sits on the floor—
*Matisse on Art,*
*Emily Dickinson,*
*The Grace in Dying.*

**Awareness**

Common is the robin redbreast,
but stately—rust red breast,
charcoal head, back, wings, tail,
black eyes, yellow pointed beak,
black and white striped neck,
an elegant palette.

Common is the gray squirrel,
but smart—a pesky character
who zips across the lawn
as fast as Zorro's sword,
finagles his way into
squirrel-proof bird feeders,
beyond baffles and up greased poles.

Common are the daily moves we make,
but divine—hugging a friend,
drinking a cup of tea,
passing through a doorway.

## Miracles

My husband brought me lilacs—
that first lusty scent of spring—
from neighbors' shrubs.
Ours always failed.
This morning I walked
across newly mown grass
to greet our first lilacs to bloom—
jubilation shared
with a rare monarch butterfly.

      *

The other day a woman
stopped me in the supermarket,
and handed me three red roses
wrapped in cellophane.
She said she already had three roses,
received from a woman handing them out
in front of the market.
Upon exiting the store I looked around.
There was no rose lady.

      *

I ask myself why, this year,
the serviceberries appear fuller,
the clouds disappearing
behind Shellhouse Mountain feel fluffier,
the ravens soaring above, look loftier,
the sky over Lake Champlain looms larger,
the sunset behind the Adirondacks seems showier,
and the autumn blaze that replaced
the storm-damaged catalpa stands statelier.

**Ordinary Day**

Take any day—
moments tick away.
Like water dripping on a rock
they slide past unnoticed.
I am distracted—
a cousin diagnosed with cancer,
a friend I haven't heard from,
a painting not coming together.

Moment creeps right up
and taps me on the shoulder.

Then I feel the crunch of gravel under my feet,
hardhearted intrusions slowing my stride,
the sun warming my back
like a heated house on a frigid day.
I see wisps of clouds stretch like thin taffy
across cobalt skies and five crows
looping on high completing the circle.

**Shellhouse Mountain**

In back of my house,
Shellhouse Mountain—
we climbed it once—
looked out over
the wide Champlain Valley.

Carved cliffs, craggy face,
hidden in summer under its green dress,
snow covering its winter nakedness,
red-tailed hawk soaring above,
ravens raucously caucusing there—
pines silhouetting its mount
on a moonlit night.

We call it *The Cathedral*.

**Hardy Pleasures**
(on an autumn drive through the Northeast Kingdom of Vermont)

A white-haired woman in a purple sweater, one hand
on each sidebar, drops heavily to her garden kneepad,
snips brittle flowers returning to their source.

A second stalwart woman in her garden,
prunes ornamental grass,
reminding me my perennials await a gentle hand.

Another hale woman turns over bronze soil
with a shovel, praising the earth,
preparing for next season's growth.

A barefoot lady curtsies to autumn,
hangs wash, gazes soft-faced at her family's clothes
set free in the breeze.

A white-bearded man in tan suspenders,
bends into winter, loads logs with a younger fellow,
celebrating strength and warmth for another year.

Cornstalks stand in a field, a season's work gone by.
Brown rot creeps up their core.
Silk tassels catch the sun.

White hydrangeas, bulbous and bountiful
hang low—senesce pink—
like snowballs on our hill.

Maples thrust their ruddy
copper and orange leaves—
embrace me on this Green Mountain pass.

Communities of pumpkins,
buxom and cherubic,
lie eager warming in the sun.

The swell of smoke from chimneys exudes a woody aroma.
Cozy fires comfort families in modest homes—
my family in the Catskills on cold summer nights.

Houses whisper neighborliness,
side by side, knowing
winter's song clamors for attention.

A brook meanders roadside where two Mergansers
splash—where a child can sit in solitude—
breathe deeply and refresh her faith.

**Late September Walk**

The Queen Anne's Lace has closed up shop,
the sun has lost its summer strength,
yellow butterflies flutter low on the driveway,
grasshoppers saw their plaintive song,
chicory and red clover cling to the side of the road.

Carl waves from his blue pickup,
glad for one more ordinary day,
thirty percent chance to beat his cancer.
Mary, from her garden, mourns her lost pasture,
gone back to trees and shrubs.
Becky, young lawyer from the end of the road,
grins, riding by, kayak tied to her wagon—
limited in knowing how days are numbered.

A monarch butterfly grazes my right shoulder,
a south wind ruffles the dead corn stalks—
its tassels sparkle in the late September sun,
a crow caws on top of the hickory.

I know this landscape.
It is my own.

**Behold**

The aloe plant, the one Holly left
when she went out west,

has found a home
in my sitting room,

sponging up southeast light,
outgrowing its large pot

again. Its spikes lavishly grow
out of six centers,

proudly upright. Flecks
of light green

patter the highways
of its verdant stems.

How perfectly
the barbs bordering its stalks

are spaced—such symmetry.
A Russian housekeeper

ate its stalks like celery.
Is Mt. Carmel more magnificent?

## Mothers

Through the telescope
in my living room
I see a doe
under the weeping willow
in the meadow below.

She stares straight at me,
her soulful brown eyes alert.
I see the wetness of her nose.
Her oval ears stretch and point
skyward—listening, vigilant.
She has heard a noise.

Her two spotted fawns,
are bedded down nearby
in the verdant grass—
so tender, defenseless,
innocent, unaware.

*Yes! Yes!*
I cry out to her.
*Take them!*
*Wrap them in your arms!*
*Run for safety!*
*Head for the woods!*
*Build a house of bricks!*

## Ravens

For years I've searched,
hoping each crow I saw
was a raven.

Mystery marks
their well-oiled bodies—
brazen ravens who belong
to night, to moonlight—
cloudy and obscure.

I, too, travel in moonlight,
in inky purple skies
*in darkness over the surface
of the deep* as Genesis says.

Ravens will offer me secrets
behind silhouetted trees,
guide me to other worlds.

One gray day
on my morning walk,
I knew instantly—
on top of the hickory—
their shocking size,
their buxom beaks,
their guttural cries—
two ravens.

One flew off
then the other—
taking me with them.

**Crone**

I bought a stuffed doll, a witch,
with a box of Barricini's chocolate
on Halloween a few years ago.
Her skin is emerald green; her nose is hooked;
her lips are red. She wears a black dress,
a pointed black hat, and purple shoes.

I wanted this crone.
I am becoming her,
*a withered old woman*
the dictionary says.
She is at home on my bookshelf.

She rides her broom through dark nights,
flies in the face of the wind like Wonder Woman,
her black hair flowing in the breeze, black eyes alert.
She invites young ones to ride with her,
like children on the back of their mother's bicycle.
She tenders sweet dreams to all below.
The moon and stars are her angels.
They tell her stories.
She knows the meaning of *uphold*.

## The Sounds of Water

Lying in bed at night
beneath the down comforter—
outside the rain, water dripping
in puddles from the roof.
Does the frog listen
under his toadstool?

Sitting on the deck
at night—stars sprinkled
like gold dust in the sky,
and the lake
gently lapping on shore.
Does the turtle hear it
under his shell?

Paddling the kayak
at dawn, water dripping
off the oar, one side,
then the other.
Does the heron hear it
under his hood?

Walking on the beach
at daybreak, ocean cresting,
breaking over sand.
Does the crab listen
under his shell?

Walking on the road
after rain, leaves
showering raindrops in the wind.
Can you hear the water
talking?

**Say, Have You Seen the Sumac?**

Along the road red-winged blackbirds twitter
among thin trunks of staghorn sumac

that undulate, dance, and spread skyward—
scruffy branches praising God.

In summer its sweet svelte leaves line up
in symmetry like a team of rowers' oars.

Cone-shaped clusters of fuzzy red berries
shoot for sun-drenched clouds.

Late in autumn its leaves hang languidly—
orange, scarlet, purple—a final chorus of color.

Even the invasive sumac shows its place
in the scheme of things.

## Spring Walk

On the side of the driveway
a dragonfly lights on gravel,
a monarch butterfly on a daisy.
A bumble bee straddles purple clover
then zigzags on his way.
Buttercups bounce sunlight
off small petals.

Down on the road, the few trees
cast their morning shadows,
leaves lifting lightly.
An Eastern kingbird
swings on milkweed,
a red-winged blackbird
saws his melody on a blade of grass.

I walk on with my Dalmatian,
glad when a newly arrived cloud
hides the heat of the sun.
Wouldn't it be nice to walk
on a tree-lined road my sweaty body
complains. But I refuse to give up
my gratitude to the heat.

## Mutual Refreshment

The hairy woodpecker hangs upside down
on the suet cage, comfortable on his trapeze.
Pointed head, pointed beak, gawk left, gawk right.
He swings and pecks, partakes of seed,
a circus clown outside my window.

Bright yellow goldfinch in black tuxedos,
perch and spar. One withdraws, the other pecks.
Seeds fly, cling to the window,
fall to the gravel. The other returns
to spar then peck like young men at an elegant ball.

The ground-feeding cardinal visits
our feeder so long as we, inside, don't move.
Black eyes under combed crest
warily watch. He pecks, he eats—
a haughty carving, a king on his throne.

Black-capped chickadees, not scared off,
hop on the window feeder,
jump in the tray, look left, look right,
peck, bang, fly off to a tree to eat their seed,
leaving their trail of energy behind.

These high-flying friends, stage their acts
as though they are professionals.

**On My Knees**

digging dandelions
from my flower garden,
early morning breeze,
hums of a distant world,
a grasshopper lopsided
on a blade of grass,
a camouflaged frog
stock still nearby,
a chickadee chants *fee-bee*
high in the hickory.

Uncle Irv appears to me
in his tan shorts,
tank top undershirt,
old brown dress shoes muddied,
chewed cigar in one hand,
pulled weeds in the other.
*If you don't get the root out,
the weed will grow back!*

Grateful for his training
I rest my eyes
on the orange brilliance
of the marigolds,
inhale their feisty fragrance,
dead head their bygone sisters,
and dig deep.

**T'ai Chi with Gray Catbird**

Now, each morning, when I do T'ai Chi
   I look for the catbird outside on
      the Harry Lauder walking stick.

He's the Cadillac of birds:
   sleek, slate gray body, black crown,
      long tail, narrow beak, coal black eyes,

larger than the perky chickadee,
   smaller, more streamlined,
      than the chunky grosbeak.

He lands on the undulating branch,
   ever vigilant—dives into the vagrant shrub,
      rustling its floppy leaves, emerges again,

looks straight at me—our eyes engage—
   watches as I move my arms around,
      rock back and forth, from side to side.

No matter the time—earlier or later,
   he is there and I'm amused,
      sharing this moment with my little friend.

I think he comes each day because
   he feels my energy,
      the connection between us.

This morning he came with a buddy,
   jumped frenetically from branch to branch,
      then flew off to another universe,

never looking back.

**Words in the Time of the Pandemic**

In the last week or so
certain words I met
in certain places
jumped out in front of me
like a child asking for attention

CANCELLED
stamped in big red letters over
events in the calendar in the local paper
covering over notices
of lectures plays concerts
CANCELLED

STRUGGLES    a word in an online newsfeed
Losses big and small Uncertainty    STRUGGLES
How do we choose to live
I choose gratitude every morning again and again and again

SAME BOAT   the Buddhist dharma teacher
on the tele summit says
Shift from I to we    SAME BOAT
Our neighbors get us groceries
We check on another neighbor recovering from surgery

A doctor on TV announces    I counsel families of my patients
to   SAY GOODBYE   He meant SAY GOODBYE   to your loved one
with COVID-19 going on a ventilator in the ICU
*Oh no* I cry out   those words scalding my chest
my grandma dying at 28   SAYING GOODBYE
to my mother age 2 her brother age 4

GENTLE FOOTSTEPS    come for us
In the mean-time    RESPIRE

# PEOPLE AND PLACES

**There You Were**
             for Icy

I requested, silently implored
the agency to send a nurse
of quiet temperament
whom my mother could tolerate
in her perturbed state
as my father lay dying.

And there you were,
in starched uniform with lace edges,
solid Jamaican body
taking up residence in the den,
gentle with my father,
resourceful for my mother.

There you were,
moving slowly through the shadows
of the day, carrying a handkerchief
with your Bible, sitting in a chair,
reading Scriptures, a holy woman
in the desert of our family.

There you were,
modeling tranquility and strength,
reminding me of God's presence,
taking me to a higher plane.

I cried in your arms
when I left.

## You Do What You Gotta Do
### for Dorothy

When she said, *You do what you gotta do*, she was referring
to bringing up two younger sisters after their mother died—
keeping house, sewing shirts for her father—
once a lined suit—jacket and pants.

When she said, *You do what you gotta do*, she was referring
to milking cows for twenty years, seven days a week,
in all weather, no vacations, no modern equipment—
keeping the books, throwing hay bales with her husband,
carrying his coffee thermos with a container
of milk in a bucket to our house for a visit.

When she said, *You do what you gotta do*, she was referring
to taking care of her aging father after early hours
at the bake shop—giving him lunch, doing laundry,
straightening up, taking him to the doctor, preparing his dinner.

Her father has died. He did what he had to do. Her stepson lives
in his house—in this house where she grew up.
It's his until whenever, she says lovingly. She lives down the road.
She will never leave it—this home she shared with her husband.

When she said, *You do what you gotta do*, she is referring
to rising at 4 a.m. to work at the bake shop—
making pies, cookies and bars—for as long as her boss—
her good friend—needs her. She will work for no one else.

She has never been out of New England. She knows all the locals.
Her modest home, heated with wood, satisfies her.

Her long, thick, brown hair shows signs of gray. She donated it
once to make wigs for cancer patients.
Her big hands are worn, working from that principled place—
*You do what you gotta do*—and her body follows.

**Prayer Poem for Alan**

Roots in Vermont,
hardy stock of Maine,
prayers resound for you
in these New England hills—
a prayer from bears
in their winter meditation,
a prayer from coyotes
in council in the moonlight,
from chickadees atwitter
in the brush,
a prayer from the pine forests
singing in the breeze,
from the long-lived oaks
shading you under their canopy.
Your friends make a circle,
enfold you within.
Your angels sing you
a right outcome.

**Portraits**

All afternoon I nest in the Green Mountains
Huntington Bird Museum, a modest building
tucked into the woods on a dirt road
where hundreds of lovingly carved birds
are displayed in habitat dioramas.

We are here to learn to keep nature journals,
altars to animal and plant life,
prayer books in graphite and watercolor.
Thirteen of us sit on folding chairs doing field sketches.
We draw carved birds, plants, leaves, and rocks.
Are we seeing their truth?
All afternoon I appeal to my heart:
*Guide my hand in portraying nature's bounty.*

II
The seven-year-old in the front row,
wearing a pink cotton dress, sandals and eyeglasses—
a front tooth missing, says, *Why can't we erase?*
*I want a different pencil.* When the blind contour drawing
is introduced she says, *I want to look.* Her drawings are mature
She has a discerning eye. Her mother is our instructor,

a tall, lithe, no-nonsense lady,
hair pulled back in a clip, sleeveless blouse,
cargo shorts, socks, and sneakers.
She pastes a smile on her face, gives her daughter
short answers to quiet the demand.

The eight-year-old in the back row
wears a yellow sundress; a blonde braid flows down her back.
She sits quietly next to her slender, light-haired mother.
Her drawings are rudimentary, her eye undeveloped.
Mother and daughter commune, smile encouragements
to each other.

III
All afternoon I ponder about mothers and daughters,
my mother and my daughters:

how long it took me to forgive my mother's
timidity and resignation, to enjoy
her humor, love of learning,
grace, cooking, concoctions—
how long it took for my daughters
to appreciate their own kindness,
humor, talents, resourcefulness, integrity—
how long it took me to forgive myself
for mothering mistakes.

## Heritage

*Nobody move!*

The student gunman pointed a handgun at members
of his British Literature class.

Kendrick Castillo, a fellow student, lunged at him,
took a bullet, and died.

Kendrick's father, an angel of patience and principle
and decency, called for us to love each other in his eulogy
to his only child. Said Kendrick was a selfless soul
of deep faith—filled with the good stuff.
We need more like him.

My daughter is disconcerted every time she sees a photo
or lawn sign celebrating Kendrick Castillo as a hero.

Her daughters, our grandchildren, are in fifth and sixth
grade in this school.

She drops down a well of unknown depth when she thinks
of Kendrick's parents' loss.

Kendrick Castillo, three days from high school graduation,
award winning four-year member
of the school's robotic team,
passionate about technology—
helpful and humorous, his friends said.

Courage is a trait he shared with his father.
Said if ever he faced a school shooter
he would take him down—
a premonition? A call?

*Colorado will always remember the heroism
of Kendrick Castillo,* said the Governor.

Please know his name—beyond the sun and the stars.
Please know his name. Please.


(After the shooting at Highlands Ranch, Colorado STEM
School at 1:53 p.m. on May 7, 2019)

## Mrs. Samuels

Often when I stepped into the hospital corridor I'd find Mrs. Samuels, slight, elderly, standing in front of her room or walking up and down the hallway. *How are things going*, she'd ask about my daughter, head cocked, nose pointed toward the ceiling, one arm on her hip, hospital gowns facing in opposite directions to cover her decently, yellow plastic sunglasses, a welder's type. *It's my heart*, she explained one day in the lounge. *They won't let me live alone. I've been here two months waiting for a place at the Mary Manning Walsh Home. I go there or I go home!* She sits, she walks, rests in bed, few visitors—accepting, like a turtle sleeping in the sun. When I ask her secret she tells me: *At forty-five I decided no point complaining. From then on I never have.* Ahh, Mrs. Samuels—claiming your rock like a Pilgrim—you sustain me. I love you like a daughter ought to love a mother.

## Companions

An elderly lady lumbers in, stepping rhythmically,
arm-in-arm, with her sister, her solid body bent forward.
She wears a black-beaded sweater and black skirt;
the heels of her black pumps slant in an uneven tread.
Her head is covered by a sheitl, a wig worn
by Orthodox Jewish ladies. Her face is lined;
her brown eyes pool deep.
Her sister is giving blood before surgery.

Talking with a slight accent, she charms the receptionist.
*My sister speaks Hungarian.* An interpreter is called—
no family members allowed in the interview.
Delicate questions might be posed.

Silently we sit, she waiting for her sister, I for my daughter,
also giving blood before surgery. She eats a sandwich
from her purse; I eat one from my tote.
She reads from a prayer book;
I read Emerson's essay on *Self-Reliance*.

Sitting in a hospital once more, grief strikes a chord in me
like an atonal oratorio. My daughter asked me,
more than once, how her illness affected me—
said it would be too painful for her to be in my position—
would rather be the one with the illness.
I often pray, talk to God, meditate by her hospital bed.
And sometimes my heart just shuts down.

The nurse appears. *Your sister is fine. Your daughter, too.
They are drinking orange juice and soon will be out.
Here are guidelines for home.*

My companion turns to me. *Life, life.* She shakes her head.
*What is wrong with your daughter?* "She has Crohn's Disease."
*So young. She will be well.*
*I'd put my hand in the fire for my sister but I couldn't be
her interpreter. She'll be shocked at the questions!*

We laugh. And the draft in the hallway
becomes a fresh spring breeze.

**Exemplary Lives**
>for Bernard & Doris

The small trailer is lined up next to its sisters,
cozy and clean. Coffee is brewing in the pot.

Now a neighbor drops by.
Now the mother bathes the schizophrenic daughter.

Now the nurse comes to check her medication.
She has become agitated again.

Now the daughter lies in the back of the van,
for an outing to the shopping mall with her parents.

Now the babysitter comes to watch the daughter
so the parents can go to the buffet at *Gloria's.*

This has gone on for more than forty years.
Never mind the grief curling out of the house.

Talk to these folks. They listen. And in their slow manner
of speaking, they may even tell you an off-color joke.

**Wait Awhile**
                for Sam Fogel

*Wait awhile,* he said,
clearing the moment to make his point.

He was a small man
carrying an old leather briefcase.

He was a rabbi, but not a rabbi,
from a family of rabbis,

a heretic who believed,
carrying his prayer book for non-believers,

an ecumenical, an ambassador,
carrying instructions for the world,

a soft voice in the ether
carrying words of compassion,

a lighthouse, a beacon
carrying a poster for peace,

a poet and a walker
between heaven and earth.

He was our friend—
a persistent journeyman until the end.

## Displaced

You could spot her, tall and graceful,
walking down the sidewalk
of her small Vermont town,
cowboy hat angled on her head.
Her snowshoes knew her well.
Her swimsuit molded her trim figure
on Town Beach.

Now, at 90, she is moored
in a senior living complex.
Her adored place over the Old Brick Store
is rented to someone else.
Her life on Cliff Island, Maine,
gathering place for seven children
and grands, has ceased.

Suddenly stymied by diminished eye sight—
she wears sunglasses—light is the culprit—
looking like a celebrity lying on her bed,
or walking with her walker.

She sees shadows again,
the deep, dark waters of herself at five,
when her parents died of pneumonia,
her mother first, then her father.
Raised by her aunt and uncle,
no one told her what happened,
as though she would not notice,
sparking a life-long search for truth—
reading, studying, writing poems and hymns,
corresponding with her spiritual lights.

She still leans in to me with love
from the ocean of her heart.
At each meal she eats a few spoonsful—
feasts now on the fruits
of other peoples' stories.
Stories. Stories.
*Tell me more stories,* she says.

**Visit with Carolyn**

*Things are changing for me,* she said yesterday.
*It all started when I turned 90.*

She is as thin as a praying mantis,
walks awkwardly with unmatched canes.

*I went to a naturopath to keep my children happy, not to a doctor who will send me for tests. And, oh, she touched my body. It was lovely.*

Her digestion is problematic, her hip misaligned,
her eyesight hazy.

*I don't go to choir anymore. It was my life
but I can't keep up with the new director.*

She wrote poetry, sang her sweet hymns
with the choir.

*I don't believe in religion's myths as the truth.
I am vertical in my spiritual life, not horizontal.*

She studied Gurdjieff, listens to audios
of Ken Wilbur and Neale Donald Walsch.

*My work now is to be loving to my family and friends.
I don't live in my mind anymore. I live in my soul.*

She is my praying mantis,
mediating between heaven and earth.

## At The Memory Unit

*Tell me where I am,* Carolyn says. *I feel like I'm in an institution.* You're in a nice place, I say. *Oh, then I'm very happy for myself.* Another move was necessary. She was wandering around nude at night. *I'm nuts,* she says. *You sound good today,* I reply. *You have lived a good life.* Her children read her stories, stories she wrote. *It clears my mental fog. I'm happy I wrote them. My children are grateful, too. Those days are history now. Words are important—more important than pictures.*

## Telling Stories

I visit Carolyn at Meadows 243 in the memory unit, a pleasant apartment off a pleasant lounge area where a few folks sit on a couch staring at a TV. She is fresh from her body massage. Lying back on her sofa she administers some eye drops. *Is this your first time here?* she asks. *Do you know I went crazy? It was due to medication. Art insisted on staying here with me even though guests may not sleep over. Now I'm OK, but my memory is gone. So I just have to say that to people.* I tell her stories about my grandchildren. *Family is so important,* she muses. *I have a friend here,* she tells me. *She was married to a doctor. She doesn't speak. But we love each other. We look into each other's eyes and we know we love each other. If you asked Andrea about me she wouldn't know who you were talking about.* I tell her a story of a woman whose Buddhist practice sustained her through the loss of her husband to Alzheimer's. *What a bee—utiful story,* she breathes. Her eyes are closed. She is resting in the light.

## Coming Up on 91

When I knock and enter Carolyn is resting in bed wearing a long sleeve shirt, wool vest, pants, and socks under her covers. Much of her lunch remains on her tray—a pile of peas, rice, chicken pieces, and fruit salad. Her gangly arms reach for her phone and walker. She wants to sit with me in the living room. She lies down on the couch. I cover her with an afghan. But soon she is cold; her feet are cold. It is 84 degrees outside. We return to her bedroom. *Tell me how things are going for you,* she says. *In relationships people should be able to say how they feel. I see it as a folding fan. Each piece spells LOVE. L is for love all the time and E for the opposite. When I'm with people I like to talk about these things.* I tell her several stories. Her eyes are closed. I talk loudly. She is deaf in one ear. Occasionally she winces. *You are talking too loudly,* she finally says. *I can hear you when you talk this softly;* she demonstrates. I ask about the photo of her seven children. *Is George the one with the beard? I don't remember,* she says. *I have no visual memory. If I see you I recognize you.* Her son Art calls. *I'm visiting with a friend,* she tells him. *I don't know. I'll have to ask her. What's your name again?* she asks me. She tells him, asks him to call later, hangs up. *Oh, I should have asked Art if George is the one with the beard. Tell the nurse she can come in anytime with my eye drops or anything else. I'm surprised no one has been in here yet.* She is tired. Our visit is over. I sigh, relieved. I am tired, too.

## In the Moment

I walk down long hallways of green carpet and yellow walls on the way to the memory unit—past doors sporting tidy flowered wreaths, an attempt at good cheer. Memories of my mother's sad time in these places surface. I stop at Carolyn's door, moved by the photo of her with husband Frank on Cliff Island in earlier days. Carolyn is waiting for me in bed. She follows me into the living room with her walker—wants to turn on lights—even the goose neck lamp over her keyboard—which reflects only on her music. She wants to make it cheerful for me. She opens a window shade, then hikes up her sweat pants before sitting down. She is thinner than last time. Her hair is plastered down with a middle part. *I'm not dressed up enough for you,* she reflects. We sit facing each other, her head resting on the back of the couch. I tell her stories—my task, more and more, at each visit which I, as an introvert, find more and more draining. She says little, smiles approvingly as I tell her about the visit of my nephew and his boys. Her eyes are slits, her mouth closed. *Are you tired?* I ask. *No. Why did you ask me that? Your eyes are almost closed,* I say. *Oh, you think there is something wrong with my eyes,* she retorts. *No. I thought maybe you wanted a nap,* I reply. *I was enjoying your stories and now there is something wrong with me,* she says with increasing agitation. *Your head is resting on the back of the couch. Maybe that's why your eyelids seemed closed,* I observe. *Oh!* She sits up, alert. Her blue eyes open wide. *There is something wrong with me!* she repeats. I search my brain for another story to distract her. She calms down some, but her eyes dart to and fro anxiously unfocused. I tell her more stories, repeat details, lean in to see if she is following. She murmurs a few words here and there. *It is time for my eye drops,* she says. I stand up, lean over, kiss her soft cheek, and look into her eyes. *Thank you for the visit,* she says. *I hope you will come again soon. I loved your stories. I will,* I automatically reply. I love her; I don't want to abandon her. But I am, once again, exhausted by the visit—drained of energy from sustained monologues. And suddenly I know I cannot come again. She rises. *You don't have to get up,* I say. *I want to see you to the door.* I turn, blow her a kiss. She returns it. Gently I close the door.

**You Took Us In**

Driving down Maple Avenue
on Christmas Eve,
singing Christmas carols
with the radio,
the street shining, wet with snow,
Christmas trees composed
inside living room windows,
Christmas lights climbing bushes,
swirling around trees, dripping off roof gutters,
reindeer and sled sculptures residing on lawns,
red and green lights blinking everywhere.

At the party, Sally's best silver,
home baked ham, salads,
pudding, pies, fruitcake,
Christmas cookies and eggnog,
their tree fanned out, floor to ceiling,
bursting with bulbs.
Tomorrow three generations
will open the gaily-wrapped presents.

*What do you do for Christmas?*
people ask me.
*Are your children coming home?*
*Do you have your tree yet?*
*Have you bought all your presents?*

I exchange holiday cards
with friends and neighbors.
Once in while a religious one arrives,
with a cross, the mention of their Savior,
and once in a while it's a Chanukah card,
reminding me of the outsider that I am.

**History Lesson**

Third desk, first row,
I vacantly scrape the label off
an aspirin bottle housing a supply of ink,
shrinking my skeleton into my seat
to avoid being called upon
to regurgitate facts
swimming around in my brain,
uninspired, dead.

American History Regents class,
Mr. Berman droning on,
joyless cog in the education wheel.
Curled lip, owlish face, darting eyes.

*We ought to put a bomb under Miss Klein,*
he suddenly roars, eyes glowering like jets,
standing tall, arrogant, irritated,
behind his desk.

Third desk, first row,
I suck in my breath, heart racing,
eyes staring wildly at this fury of a man.
Startled, humiliated, riveted to my seat
like a statue, I want to run.
Nursing my wound privately,
no words form, trained not to make waves.
No skills in place to address such rudeness.

Slowly a question forms.
*And what, may I ask, are you teaching,*
*Mr. Brown Suit history teacher?*
*What kind of history are you making?*

## Kindergarten Teachers

Grace Gilmore sat at her desk,
shading her ice blue eyes with her hand,
alone in her unlit classroom,
when the children had not yet come,
or had just gone home—
sat in the gray silence
that filled the unoccupied spaces of the room.

And I, next door in my classroom,
the other kindergarten teacher,
newly appointed,
young, energetic, creative—
privately scoffed
at this slightly odd spinster,
whose eyes never softened into the present.

Grace Gilmore sat at her desk,
shading her ice blue eyes with her hand,
alone in her unlit classroom,
when the children had not yet come,
or had just gone home—
sat in the gray silence
that filled the unoccupied spaces of the room.

Now I, the mother of growing children,
sit at my desk,
alone in my unlit bedroom,
when the family has gone for the day,
and feel the caress of the gray silence
that fills the unoccupied spaces of the room.
And in that enchanting stillness
I listen to the rhythms of my heart.

Grace Gilmore, I apologize.
I salute you, my sister.

## Waiting for a Procedure

The elderly man in the next bay
talks haltingly in a tired, husky voice,
hesitant in the face of all this medical rigmarole.
He left his dentures and hearing aids at home.
Hasn't used them in quite some time.
*They need adjustment and new batteries*, he says.
He's bleeding internally.
They can't find the source.

In my bed, tucked in with warmed blankets,
I am reading Donald Hall's *Claims for Poetry*.
*Do I need to hear that man's personal information?*
I ask my prep nurse when she comes back.
*That's more information than I should have,* I say.
*There's an issue about privacy here,* she agrees.
*You can put it in a poem.*

**Mobile**
      for Suzanne Hindle  (1944-2019)

Sitting straight in her wheelchair
in her mountain cabin in New Mexico
where she came for the climate
when her body was giving out,
blanket covering legs
used to carrying her
to human resources work in DC,
brown eyes alert—
ready to engage—
with a visitor, a movie, a book,
a tasty meal, her devoted cats—
platinum white hair
hanging straight, swinging
around her ears when she laughs,
a warrior like Christina in Andrew Wyeth's
painting, that painting which always intrigued her.

She knows her arm muscles
are weakening.
She knows her caretaker
is getting old.
She knows but does not dwell on it.

She knows she is more than a body.
She knows there is something else.
She knows the sounds and sights of *Her* castle,
and smiles that smile—of gratitude and joy,
so captivating to her many friends
who cherish her spirit.

After she died we each received
a picture from her art card collection—
how did she know of my love
for northern latitudes—
mine a crisp lake embraced
by thin-spiked pine trees,
dotted with snow remnants on the far shore,
comforted by a mountain
off in the horizon.

**Northern Latitudes**

After experiencing Scotland,
I hankered for its Orkney Islands,
those mostly uninhabited windswept rocky islets
with names like Muckle Skerry,
Sule Skerry and Holm of Scockness,
where craggy coastlines and remote beaches
host great black-backed gulls
that soar on thermals and updrafts,
and arctic terns, bobbins, and puffins
breed among weather beaten stones and cliffs.

After scrutinizing Emily Carr's paintings
in Ottawa I fancied a spell
in her Canadian wilderness where
the moon speaks down from a purple sky,
Indian totems glower by the forest's lair,
where pine trees bristle,
moss chases round tree trunks,
and pine needles crunch
beneath the feet of the rare visitor.

After visiting Ely, Minnesota
I coveted time
in the Boundary Waters Canoe Area Wilderness,
a primitive vastness
of forests, glacial lakes, and streams,
where Dorothy Molter—a nurse and root beer
lady for summer canoeists—lived on Knife Lake,
mostly alone, for fifty-six years.

Up there in those northern latitudes
I imagined
catch-your-breath fresh air,
music of wind song and birdsong,
the pristine earth saying yes,
offering a crisp awakening, wising my bones.

**In the Champlain Valley**

If you want to behold

Tom Turkey strutting and fanning
round his seven ladies of the field,

the evening grosbeak cracking seeds
in its hefty beak on the window birdfeeder,

the moose and her yearling, heads aloof,
sniffing and grazing in the brush,

the plush peonies thrusting
their startling pink fragrance,

the stocky woodcock,
probing the driveway,

the black bear cub clumsily
clambering up the ash tree,

the great horned owl in the inky dusk,
stealthily watching from the barn roof,

the vigilant bobcat
sneakily stalking the woodlot,

the apricot sunset slowly sliding down
behind purple silhouette mountains,

the screaming crimson of the autumn blaze
in its final riotous act,

the sun singing glory
on glimmering iced tree branches,

the white fog
loving the snow-capped trees,

the packed earth talking
to your feet with every step you take,

you know then,
you must choose this place and stay awhile.

## Architecture for the Soul

An open-weave, outdoor room,
my childhood in the country—
in the Catskills—
we called it the *Tea House*—
white pine lattice boards,
a criss-crossing pattern.
Vines crept up its sides
across the roof.
Irregular flagstone shapes,
a grand puzzle, made the floor.
It was an airy room, for angels,
fairies, and family festivals.
People promenaded
from Seurat's Sur La Grande Jatte.

II
An archway, a trellis, a passage,
my elder years in the country—
in the Champlain Valley—
cedar logs network—
perpendicular, diagonal,
Adirondack style—
sit on a gravel bed
with a red brick border.
Duvas and doves
go in and out,
weave garlands of gardenias
from secret gardens,
watch friends and lovers,
dreamers and dawdlers,
prophets and poets
pass through this sacred space,
on their way to who knows where.

## Reflections on Lake Champlain

The engine purrs. I feel the boat's
rhythm and sway. Its flags wave lustily
in the wind. It is not summer
without a ferry ride to Essex for dinner
on the water, another opportunity
for time on Lake Champlain.
I sink into the bench on the upper deck,
curl into my husband's side,
watch tourists below, enjoy tranquil views—
cormorants drying spread wings
on dock stanchions, gulls circling, crying,
small forested islands thrusting up
from the lake, quaint buildings
and rolling farm land dotting the far shore,
white sails billowing here and there
as sailboats heel.
My peaked hat shades my eyes
from the sun lowering in the western sky,
glistening on undulating waves,
an orange fireball releasing
pink and purple vapors.

Looking out in the distance
I suddenly reflect on an image
from the past—the Revolutionary War,
fought on this sacred lake—
fleets of boats, cannons firing,
the wounded, the dead, liberty at stake.
And I wonder how we will fare
in the next two hundred thirty-five years.

I pray the setting sun spreads a calm,
each rising sun becomes a soothing balm—
circles of light, of lovingkindness—
that warms our children's hearts so oneness
replaces differences between *them* and *us*,
intertwined as we are,
like the braided rope connecting our ferry
with the shore.

**Island Mentality**

Another occasion for me to go,
leave my mainland mind behind,
absorb sparse culture—
distilled activity—
where wrinkled women meditate
on decades of craft,
screen doors bang,
sweaty bodies labor on bicycles
past white fences dripping with rose hips,
where beachcombers with buckets
collect prized shells,
sandpipers scurry,
resolute walkers trace bluffs
between weathered houses
and scintillating sea.

Motors rev,
the ferry departs,
fog horns blare,
gulls swirl and cry.
Curled on a wooden bench,
I languish over the rail,
dazzled by glimmering ocean,
transported by windless water—
and exude from every pore,
the hot orange and purples
of Gauguin's Tahiti shore.

## Island Life

We wait for the ferry to Burton Island.
Families unload camping gear on the dock.
I envy their days on the island.
We have but a few hours.

Burton Island—boats in the marina,
families swim, ride bikes on gravel roads,
eat ice cream at picnic tables
outside the snack bar.

We walk the trails, sheltered by sumac,
maple, and shaggy bark hickory,
shoulder-height goldenrod and wild bergamot.
I step into the moment.

At the south end
a couple sits on camp chairs,
the Green Mountains and Adirondacks
in the distance.

We sit on a rock,
watch sailboats,
motor boats, ply the lake,
listen to gently lapping water.

Like swaying in a hammock,
swaying back and forth,
my body gratefully slows
to the rhythm.

## On Top of Whiteface Mountain

On top of Whiteface Mountain we can see for twenty miles. Strong wind tousles our hair. Lake Placid below holds two big islands and a tiny third—purple mountain ridge lines 360 degrees around. On the platform, a guide—arms spread out on the corners of the deck—embraces his world with pleasure and comfort, crocodile hat tied under his chin, large, thick glasses—a plump, friendly sort. He answers our questions: *What's the farthest visibility? What peak is that? How is this weather station accessed in winter? What is that bird? Which are the Greens?* Another couple stops, asks a question, joins our group. He, a border guard, helicopter pilot—a tall, thick man with a ready, broad smile tells us many tales—one tumbling out after another—about tracking and intercepting illegal immigrants and drug dealers easily stealing our Canadian borders—hiding a distance from checkpoints, using brush as a camouflage. On top of Whiteface Mountain—one of the high Adirondack peaks—two men in their *right livelihood* as taught by the Buddha.

## Open Mic at Carol's Hungry Mind Cafe

There were six sign-ups. Keith was in charge. It was early.
He opened with smooth country—
*Goodnight Irene* on his tenor guitar.

We were next, half a dozen strong—leading gaily with ukuleles
and song, taking joy where it ought to go.
*Ukulele Lady* never had it so good.

Eric said he was happy to be among us with his new eight-string
baritone guitar. He peered over it—absorbed by his composition—
a flamenco player's dream.

Robert, the Waldorf School teacher—steady, smiling, strumming
his guitar—told us about William, a difficult autistic child, who,
one day, wowed the school, singing *Country Roads*—
like Robert does now.

John, the quiet café owner, struck the first chord on his guitar—
instantly commanding. I sat up straight. He sang *King of the Road*
and we knew he was.

Joey, oh, Joey, the college freshman, stood, seemingly timid.
With nary a glitch, body gesticulating, voice rising and falling—
faster, slower—he recited by heart—
Mark Strand, Margaret Atwood, Sylvia Plath, Patricia Smith,
and his own *Politics and Prisms*.

Nellie sang two songs—one short, one long, oh, so long—
songs by her favorite songwriter. She sang a cappella
in a high clear voice, her eyes focused on something—
something out there in the universe. Patting the air with one hand,
she noted pauses, holding a small book in the other
to remind her of words she knew by heart, as though
they were her daily guide.

All night long I had the feeling I was in a temple.

## At the Annual Town Meeting in Ferrisburgh, Vermont

Couples sit close together on folding chairs
in the elementary school cafeteria
hunched over the town report
as each article and budget item
is raised for discussion by the moderator.
One occasionally whispers in the other's ear.
The other nods or whispers a response—
that certain intimacy—after years of marriage—
that shared history no one else can be privy to—
that candle lit together long ago—
that same continuity between family members,
longtime friends.

When I talk with those I know for many years—
talk that same tongue—of people, places,
stories shared, it is comfort and consolation I feel.

And when the great waters that have
protected and proclaimed these alliances,
provided boats for the journey,
calls the other home, and I am left,
moored alone, plying life's byways,
in the silence I can hear them.

**At the Yarn Shop**

Yarn over,
slip a stitch.
Grandmothers tell stories,
sit at the table,
stoke ancient fires.

Yarn over,
knit two together.
Spider women knit their web
with vigor and fortitude,
share secrets of the sisterhood.

Yarn over,
knit to the end.
Emily, the young one, learns
the craft, inherits the code.
Elders smile.

Yarn over,
work even.
Bind off.
Attach a border.
Frame a life.

## At Harry's Bar in Gainesville, Florida on New Year's Eve

Across from us a husband and wife sit
next to another man. They have been drinking.
The single man and the wife talk
and laugh together. Her husband
lays his head on her shoulder
pretending to enjoy the interchange.

Three women sit at the end of the bar
in cocktail dresses—two talk to each other—
the third stares into space.
Why am I thinking they are wishing for a man?

The woman with the black dress and shawl,
frizzy black hair parted in the middle,
red lips and satisfied, demure air—reminds me
of a Flamenco dancer—and Frieda Kahlo.
Her escort—a small man, slightly balding,
with a thin moustache—the only man
in suit and tie—her partner in dance,
pleased and pleasing her with his stories.

I eat my Creole soup and Bayou shrimp
and sip my Blue Moon beer.

## Birding on the Gulf Coast

Haughty, debonair wading birds—
blue and green herons, ibis,
snowy and great egrets—
declare themselves hunchbacked citizens
of our patio—undulating necks rising
out of feathered suits.
Long, skinny legs move—houses on stilts.
Long, sharp beaks—straight and curved—peck.
They come to the glass door, eyes alert,
asking for food. We throw them pieces
of ham, shrimp, salmon.

I spy an amorphous shape out on the dock stanchion.
Is it a speckled rock, furry pillow, clay sculpture?
Head and throat tucked under feathers,
a brown pelican emerges, like a rabbit out of a hat.
He stretches, points his gullet to the sky, gulps,
then splash—dives for prey.

Me, a northern birder, first time on Lemon Bay.
Is he there for me?

## Morning Walk on the Gulf Coast

Shaded by languid Spanish moss
draped on towering oak branches
and palm fronds poked by the breeze,
I walk in this neighborhood of manicured lawns.

I pass an elderly gentleman
hanging out his American flag.
Overcome with gratitude
I nod good morning,

my hands engaged by walking poles.
He salutes me, bowing slightly
from the waist.
I smile at the debonair veteran

I imagine him to be
and the gladdening morning.

## The Gulf Coast in Winter

My morning walk—
a man in black shorts,
black sweatshirt,
and black cabbie hat
sails by on his bicycle,
a long cigar
protruding from his lips.

A high sun glistens
on palm leaves
that fan out like grass skirts
in the Gulf breeze.

A snowy egret casually steps
between two pygmy palms
to let me pass.

Songbirds twitter and chirp,
high on the zigzag branches
of pine trees—
blue sky juts through.

I pass a sign
tacked to a mammoth oak tree
dripping with moss.
*Keep Out!* it says.
But how can I?

## How To Ride the New York City Subway

Swipe your metro card,
face toward you,
traverse the turnstile,
hurry to your platform,
eyes straight ahead.
When your train hurtles in,
stand aside, let passengers off,
walk quickly on, find your place.
Pretend not to watch
the Puerto Rican woman sleeping
across the way, with the Clara Bow
eyebrows, long, uneven eyelashes,
black scarf across her mouth,
the one you want to draw,
or the man in a safari sun hat
and baby blue fleece shoes,
or the Barnard student,
in a soiled, beige coat,
curly hair bolted back,
hanging onto a strap, reading
a paperback called *Pearl*,
or the seated dwarf, legs suspended
in midair, bag strapped across his chest,
hat with earlaps pulled down,
engrossed in his book.
Pretend you're not eavesdropping
on the Asian mother, eyes hidden
by a cloche hat, telling her daughter,
staring up at her through eyeglasses,
about a musical contest in which
you could make seven mistakes.

And when three Mexican musicians,
in cowboy hats and boots,
walk through the car, stop in the middle,
sing and play accordion and guitars,
everyone smiling, one unified family,
say gracias to the one who passes the hat
as you throw in a dollar.

## New York City Travel

Riding the No. 1 subway train, lost in thought, I suddenly
look up as we pull into a station. No signs are visible.
*What station is this?* I ask the young woman to my left.
She looks at me, gets up, and walks out the door.
Leaning over across the aisle, the young man wearing a kippa,
asks, *What station do you want? 231st Street* I reply.
*You have four more stops. Thank you very much*, I say.
He allows a small nod.

II
A young Asian lady in a long black dress with t-straps
sits down in the crowded subway car,
pulls a black bolero sweater from her backpack.
Sitting forward in her seat she struggles to get her arms
through the armholes, to pull the sweater down in back—
squeezed as she is—between strangers. The man to her right,
reading his newspaper, quietly reaches over,
gives the back of her sweater a tug, then returns
to his reading. She eyes him distrustfully.

III
The 96th Street Crosstown bus comes to a stop. People choke
the aisle. *Woman with a walker needs to exit*, someone shouts.
*Woman with a walker getting out. Let her through, please.
Let her through.* People standing in the aisle press back.
People standing in the front step off momentarily.
Down the center of the aisle parades
a frail lady in a tan trench coat, bent over a walker,
a tan cloth sun hat pressed firmly on her head. The driver
presses a lever. The front step becomes a ramp. She exits
and quickens her pace, exhilarated by her regal flight.

## Tiny Tales from Public School 26

Kindergarten
I was sick the day the kindergarten had their circus.
    We had been preparing for it for two weeks.
    I begged my mother to let me go.
    Girls in pinafore dresses
    with hankies pinned to their chests,
    boys in shirts and ties, donned
    handmade brown bag masks,
    became elephants, lions, clowns, acrobats
    and performed to music. There was popcorn
    and singing.
Miss Gottlieb saved me a basket of peanuts
    made of colored paper handles attached
    to paper cupcake cups, and my elephant mask,
    a disappointing end to a missed festival.
And it was beautiful Miss Havity, the other teacher
    in our double kindergarten room
    who captured my heart. Miss Havity,
    in high heels, dark hair, black picture hat,
    who sat on the piano bench where Paul,
    our precocious classmate, concertized for us,
    and told us she was leaving to get married—
    leaving me downhearted.

First Grade
Everyone laughed when Miss Tocaben, auburn hair in net,
    stepped gingerly in brown sweater and skirt,
    tied a ribbon around Barry's head
    in the basement, at recess, as we sipped
    our pint containers of milk through a straw.
I laughed too long, too hard. Did I cause a commotion?

>    She left me there, in the corner,
>    bewildered, ashamed, when our first grade
>    returned to class.

Second Grade
Happily I skipped in the old gym with the low ceiling
>    on the squeaky wooden floor
>    to *Bluebird, Bluebird, Through My Window*
>    in the old part of the building,
>    sliding partitions determining classroom boundaries.

Short, round, Miss Connelly, blond permed hair flying
>    from the center of her scalp, gray suit,
>    black, low-heeled, pointy Oxford shoes,
>    distributed creamy paste, white as snow,
>    smelling like shampoo
>    on bits of oaktag with wooden Dixie spoons.
>    We read from Dick and Jane,
>    then pasted new Dick and Jane words,
>    cut from our workbooks,
>    into black and white marbleized composition books
>    so that Dick and Jane undulated on the page
>    and crackled with excitement.

Third Grade
I won proverb contests in third grade,
>    banking a roll of life savers each time for remembering:
>    *Haste makes waste,*
>    *A bird in the hand is worth two in the bush,*
>    *A stitch in time saves nine,*
>    *A rolling stone gathers no moss,*
>    *Make hay while the sun shines.*

Tall, lanky Miss Horowitz, teacher of proverbs,

called *Horrible Horowitz*, (I held her in affection),
short, dark hair, thick eyeglasses,
one day stapled her thumb,
called me to her desk
to tie gauze around her bleeding finger,
a task much less relished than remembering proverbs.
From a tall, tin pitcher she poured watery blue-black ink
    into our inkwells
    where we dipped our pens,
    with removable nibs,
    to write our first permanent messages to the world.

Fourth Grade
Miss Nolan, red-haired, slim-suited, good-natured,
    taught fourth grade in the new wing of the school,
    took us to the new auditorium on assembly day,
    girls in white middy blouses, red ties,
    pleated, navy skirts,
    boys in white shirts and clip-on ties,
    where Miss Crantz led us in music appreciation,
    taught us singing mnemonics
    to remember compositions:
    *To a rose, to a rose, to a wild rose,*
    *by MacDowell, by MacDowell, written by MacDowell,*
where Miss Crantz criticized those with a hand on their mouth,
    singing impeded. *All hands in laps*, she shouted. My hand
    unconsciously remained. *You!* she pointed. *Get out!*
    Shocked. Color creeping up my face, I stood,
    made my way past classmates to the aisle,
    reached the cool of the hall, where dear Miss Nolan
    greeted me with compassion.

Fifth Grade
Our committee studied Ecuador for our unit on South America,
    cutting, pasting, drawing pictures of that country,
    making signs, decorating one whole corkboard panel
    between clothing closet doors at the back of the room,
    stealing looks at other panels, trying to be more creative
    Miss Hines, our fashionable young teacher, skirt to knee
    nylons, high heels, sat at her desk, eating an orange,
    painting her fingernails.

Sixth Grade
I turned the hand crank of the film strip projector
    frame by frame as I read *Three Billy Goats Gruff,*
    *Goldilocks,* or *Little Red Riding Hood*
    to the kindergartners,
    so small, so avidly attentive,
    as part of Miss O'Connell's sixth grade
    Visual Aid Squad.
She taught us the Charleston, the Turkey Trot,
    the Two-Step, the Black Bottom,
    those dances from the '20s and '30s
    we danced shyly with boy partners.
That spring, before graduation, we performed
    for the school.

# ARTISTS AND WRITERS

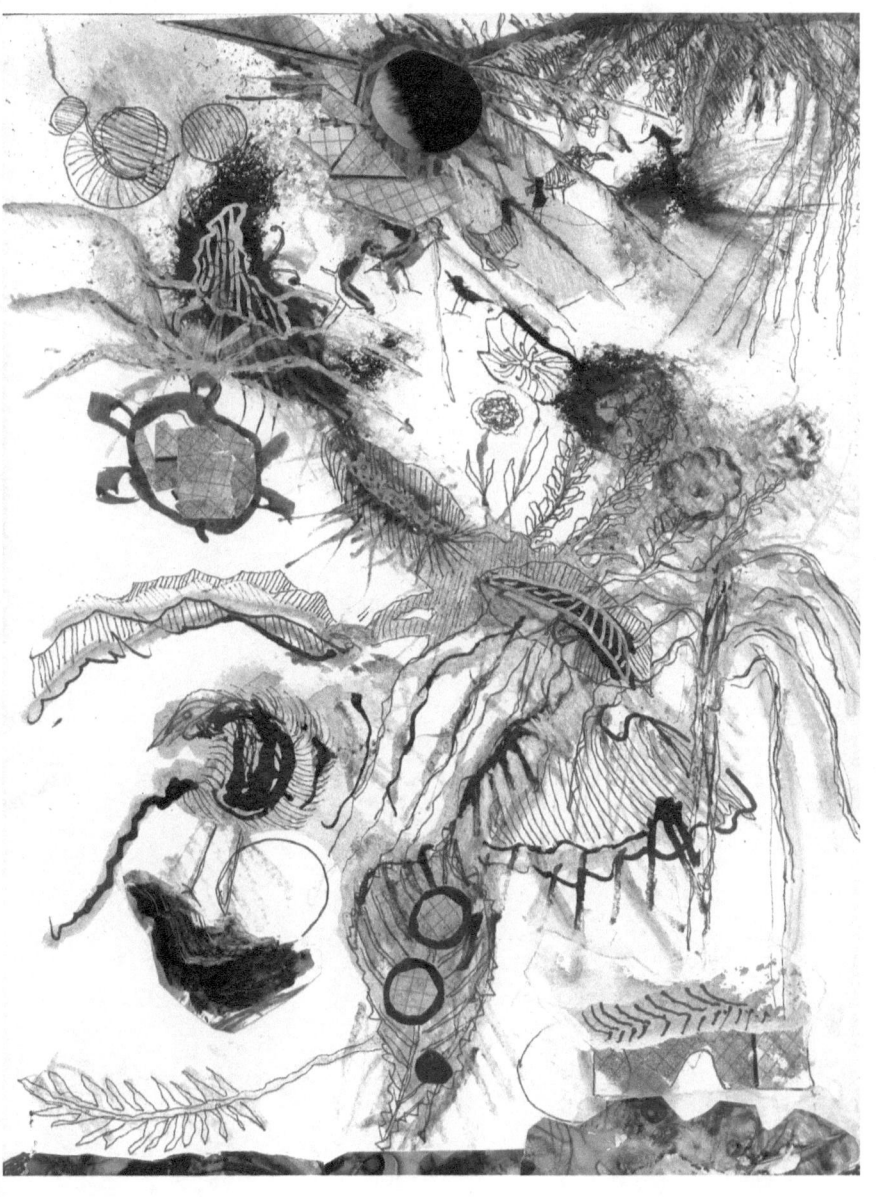

**The Red Studio**

At forty I discovered Matisse in a coffee table art book,
drinking in his paintings like a thick shake through a straw.
Fauvist colors asserted themselves—
Madame Matisse with blue hair and eyebrows,
green stripe at home in the center of her face.

Lines squiggled across canvases—
curvy odalisques reclined
on patterned beds,
beside patterned drapes,
beside patterned wallpaper—
marks romping in three-quarter time.

Paper cutouts of dancers, swimmers, and acrobats
performed in his star-filled galaxy—
in this language I knew.

Then one day I collided with a memory,
like Proust's boy delighting in petites madeleines.
At age fourteen, when I got my own bedroom,
I chose *The Red Studio* to decorate my space—
that painting in Chinese red—
with canvases hanging,
and stacked up against the wall,
with stools sporting sculptures,
a table supporting vases, glasses, plates,
a dresser holding bowls and cups—

that painting by Matisse.

And I was amazed that that fourteen-year-old
knew my sensibilities.

## A Question for Milton Avery

May I stand beside you
and watch you paint,
see how you reduce life
to simple shapes?
No need to ask,
in your portrait of March,
why your cross-legged daughter
has v-shaped arms,
elongated legs,
rectangular feet,
a diamond-shaped head,
facial features absent.

May I stand beside you
and watch you play with color—
colors a clothing catalogue
would assign exotic names?
*The Seated Blonde,*
ecru and ivory,
wearing an azure halter
sitting on an ebony chair
on a mango floor
in front of a mustard wall
with a sapphire painting
in a salmon frame
next to a fuchsia wall
behind a ruby and pewter figure—
this recipe for color,
a chef's delight.

May I stand beside you
and watch you paint?
No need to talk.
I know your native tongue.

## On Encountering Henry Moore's Sculpture

As soon as I catch a glimpse of Henry Moore's women
in any museum, I am not responsible for my behavior.
You might as well have drugged me at the door.
I want to sidle up to them like a purring cat
rubbing its side against its beloved owner's leg.
I gasp and sigh and stare, not wanting to release my gaze
from the first woman I meet, this mountainous, regal,
reclining beauty. I want to take her home.
She notices me staring. We introduce ourselves, talk.
I whisper my devotion in her ear,
compliment her on her earthy shape,
those monolithic mounds. You wouldn't have to coax me.
I'd climb up and fall asleep in the lap
of this primitive-looking broad
breathing through a hole in her middle
and take her for my mother.

**Paul Klee's Fantasmagoria**

See, Klee wasn't concerned
with conventions when he painted you,
O, sun, moon, fish, bird, snail, fruit,
O, wiggling botanicals.
He crept inside you and painted
your blooming.
How many have so honored your divinity?
Still I don't always understand you.
Pardon me for saying so.

But that day, walking slowly through the exhibit,
drinking in Klee's secret cities, gardens,
signs and symbols,
reclining on beds of softly placed color,
I said to myself:
*I don't need to understand you.*
*It is enough that Klee painted us a new language.*

## The Gentle Painter

He was a gentle giant you know—
Jacob-Abraham-Camille Pissarro.

Gentle, this man—painting in plein air
in round black hat, long sleeves, long pants,
long black cape, clogs, white beard protruding.

Gentle—notice his small, soft, brushstrokes—
droplets of love—no hard edges
in the muted greens, blues, yellows and oranges
of his landscapes and people,
cities and harbors—
beloved places others might have called ugly
he infused with light.

The upper class criticized him
for painting the common man.
Married his mother's servant.
Caused quite a stir.

*Paint generously and unhesitatingly,* he said.
*Rework unceasingly until you've got it.*

Gentle man—your deep, sunken eyes
and melancholy make no mention
of tenacity.

**Reading Gabriele Munter**

If I could read you a story of a Munter painting,
I'd read you a story of color—
a red-on-green palm tree thrusting red fruit,
a turquoise house spawning purple windows,
an orange tree among multi-green shrubs,
a pink path leading to all.

If I could read you a story of a Munter painting,
I'd read you a story of simple shapes—
oval tree tops dancing on hills,
rectangular shadows cast upon roads,
yawning houses on oblongs of grass,
triangle mountains that reach for the sky.

If I could read you a story of a Munter painting,
I'd read you a story of brush strokes thick as pudding—
streaking Marianne Werefkin's long green face,
blue-green dress, purple scarf,
the zesty flowers adorning her hat,
the yellow wall framing this friend.

If I could read you a story of Munter paintings,
I'd read you a picture book, sprightly and refreshing,
for whooping it up, singin' in the rain.

## Chagall's Dalliance

They are primitive, playful,
strange and surreal

in black strokes—
loose, thick, wispy,

and shards of color—
red, yellow, blue, and green.

They are amiable goats
and fanciful birds.

They are fiddlers, peddlers
and dallying lovers.

They are smiling donkeys
and spangled fish.

They are roosters, acrobats
and angels with bouquets.

They are tender dreams
of his Russian village.

They float festively above Vitebsk
as if that will change their reality.

It was a hard life,
but you'd never know it—

all of that mythology
impishly claiming the sky.

**My Dearest Edouard Vuilliard**

Thank you for the chance
to stay at your mother's house—
to meet the noble women in your life:
your no-nonsense grandmother,
your hard-working mother,
her dressmaking clients,
your reticent sister,
your cherished friend—
the enveloping Madame Lucie Hessel—
the busy women, quaint women, melancholy women
who inhabit your paintings—
sewing, sweeping, waiting,
visiting, eating, writing—
alone, together, in their dusky interiors—
striped wallpaper, plaid bedcovers, floral rugs—
disparate patterns that meet at their edges.
O, I do delight in resting awhile in their womanly rooms
smelling of camphor and comfrey.

## Charles Burchfield's Salem

Houses and barns huddle with grieving eyes
and gaping mouths that cry out for comfort
in this modest town.
Ballooning clouds fill stained glass skies.
The wind rains sinister icicles.
Lightning spreads a paw-like hand
in native fields and woods.
Trees reach out their arms and mysteriously
call you in. Lanky sunflowers open
one Redon eye. Violets expose screaming faces.
Seed pods yawn. Bushes swirl
in Van Gogh rhythms.
Butterflies and crickets ripple.
Sunlight streaks like skywriting trails.
Grasses grow before your eyes.
*Open, open,* he whispers
as they pass through the turnstile of his mind.

**About Franz Kline's Black and White No. 2**

He slaps broad black brush strokes, thick with verve, across generous white paper.

Two vertical lines on the left—sturdy and brash—balance one on the right.

Two horizontal lines undulate in between—forge a bridge to some brave new world.

## My Dinner in Finland

I am elegant in Vuokko's dress and cape—

> thin black lines scattered
> across generous white fabric.

I glide onto Alvar's undulating wood chair,
pour ice water from Aino's glass pitcher—

> a widening swirl—
> small gesture for a spout—

eat Karelian pasty—rice in a rye crust—
from Kaarina's porcelain plates—

> glowing translucently like a full moon
> bordered by a night sky—

cut my food with Bertel's sleek silver service,
pour currant wine from Tapio's glass carafe—

> sinewy as it tapers
> from base to neck—

feel Marjatta's woven tablecloth grazing my knees,
smile at Tyra's ceramic birds—

> sitting on their bellies,
> questioning, debonair—

pour tea from Marita's clay pot—

> spout and handle at attention,
> fat womb enthroned.

*Hail Finlandia!*

**Children of the Sun**
(after a painting by Haitian artist Prosper Pierrelouis)

Listen. The *loas* are talking.
These bright-eyed spirits
come forward with joy.
Long-armed, short-legged,
they smile and wave.
All sassy and light,
they twist and wiggle,
wedge themselves in—
five in all, some short, some tall.
Birds sail forward—
snuggle like angels—
under their arms.
Wispy vines—
orange, yellow, lime—
grow around them,
dominate their dresses—
magenta on purple,
purple on white.
Sunning snakes settle the border.
The long-armed loa
hugs a fierce Haitian sun.

**Jean Dubuffet's Transgressions**

Hey Dubuffet,

you push paint like a five-year-old,
mixing in tar, string, cement and glass—
smearing, imbedding,
scratching like a chicken—
flaunting unflattering bodies—
a red-skinned sorcerer,
a brown crustacean,
a crude portrait
of a woman in childbirth,
a lady with roasted flesh,
another hairy with yellow teeth,
a ridiculous nude trying on a hat,
five *important* businessmen eating lunch.

I'm with you, Dubuffet.
Let's jump around on the canvas,
throw sand and gravel.
Primitive, yes, primitive.
I want to paint primitive, too!

## Inuit Artists of Hudson Bay

First People are sculptors, weavers, printmakers,
dancers, drummers, and accordionists.

They are hunters, harpooners, kayakers,
ball players, and builders in all seasons.

They are walrus, whale, wolf, trout,
seal, musk ox, bear, and caribou.

They are geese, hawk, tern, raven,
owl, loon, and swan.

They are summer tent, winter tent,
spring tent, and fall tent.

They are fur-lined boots and parka,
oil stove, and kettle.

They are shamans, dreamers, mythical
creatures, animal spirits, day and night spirits.

They are my star-filled siblings
reveling, spinning round our cosmos.

They have no words for grace and joy.

## In Emily Carr's Canadian Forests

you can hear them mutter and groan—
those bold trees with gnarled trunks—
like craggy old men, who fling their branches,
quiver and thrash, reach for the sky,
and huddle in canopy.
Sunbeams sneak through to moss carpets below
rolling round tree trunks like a song.

Over there in the clearing—
below swirling sky—an Indian totem.
Bear, beaver, eagle
sneer, grimace, stare, and cry.
Listen to them whisper secrets
for no one to hear.

**Melancholy**
(after Helene Schjerfbeck paintings)

*Girl Crocheting*—1904
She sits, shrouded in a black, high-neck, long-sleeved,
floor-length dress, auburn hair pulled back,
slender body turning in on itself, arms held in close.
Large hands shield her crocheted piece;
a ball of white yarn rests gently in her lap. Head bent,
lowered eyes in her long, pale face, attend
the crochet hook and yarn, her gaze as sorrowful
as the somber wall.

*The Seamstress*—1905
She leans forward in her rocker cloaked in black dress
with high collar, black hair mounded
like a Kabuki woman. Scissors hang from her belt.
A bit of white fabric clings to the back of the chair;
hands clasp in her lap, face blanched
like an ivory cameo, downcast eyes
as quiet as the room, as quiet as winters in Finland.

*Self-Portrait*—1912
In a head pose she wears a high-collared navy blouse
short brunette hair pulled back behind her ears—
a stubborn curl—uncontrolled—protrudes.
Her white face, drawn-down cheeks,
pursed pink lips and blue eyes seem to question,
worry, fear a disturbance as she gazes
over her shoulder at someone out of view.

We don't see the limp in her gait
from a fall down a staircase at age four.
We don't know she returned to Finland
after her fiancé abandoned her in Paris.
But look again
at her portraits of women,
so styled in muted tones.

**Tulip**
(Meditation on a drawing by Ellsworth Kelly)

Go, eyes, caress the edges
of this tulip. Guide the hand
holding the pencil.
Go, hand, fingers loose,
touch the paper
naked with anticipation—
follow the petals, one, two, and three,
through curved inlets,
over mountain contours.
Slowly, slowly, meet the stem,
bending and lilting,
breathing, awake.
Keep the connection—
bring it down,
down to the first leaf standing tall,
pointing skyward, hallelujah—
down to the broader leaf
framing the first,
then to the last
across the way,
languidly curling, bending low,
touching the earth—
a rooted family.
Then bring the stem up,
home to the petals—
open to the sky—
joining, connecting.

**Swimming in Abstractions**
(after Arthur Dove's *Golden Sun* and *Moon* paintings)

I am floating
around blankets of sun.
I mean I am swimming
in Eden, protected
in this yellow ether
by warm saffron skies,
gazing down on tufted greenery,
melting into abstruseness.
Soft slanting sunbeams
sink into blue water below.
Loose, yes, loose.

I am arcing like a porpoise
around the honeyed aura
of a bright-eyed moon
in opaque green skies.
I mean I'm gliding, encircling
my glowing playmate
under cover of night,
at the center of light.
One wide sienna moonbeam
exposes dark velvet mountains below.
Loose, yes, loose.

**Tulips and Irises**
(after a painting by Emil Nolde)

loaded paintbrush wet paper
color swollen, smirking

stems bleeding into leaves
leaves bleeding into flowers

irises blending with tulips
flowing flooding

swaying, budding
brashly bursting

blurry boogy borders
seeping, searching

feeling their way
cobalt into yellow

lavender into navy
red into green into blue

coalescing cooperating
under over through

loosely lurking
wide water waltz

## Van Gogh Took His Reed Pen

and made black marks—

      horizontal, vertical,
          slanted, straight,
              curves, commas,
                  dense and light—

a flower, a cornstalk,
spiraling, swaying,
stars and moons,
houses and roads,
all in their place,
their shorthand place,
a spreading shrub,
sprouting grass,
alive, alive—
everything alive—
a grimacing tree,
bent and stooped.

With lines and dots
he sings their praises—

      daa, daa,
          daa, daa,
              daa doo.

## Zen Painting: Mu Chi'i's Persimmons

Dip, press, lift—
press, swirl, lift—
rivers of ink on rice paper.

Breath becomes form,
energy paints itself,
the universe in a line.

**Pic Island, Lake Superior**
(after a painting by Lawren Harris)

Near the shore of Lake Superior,
Pic Island, a regal brown mound—
velvet like beaver fur—
rises famously from teal blue waters.
White clouds crown the island
like a guardian from above,
join waves of lavender, sage, and blue sky—
tepid colors of the shrouded north.

I'm back again in the northern latitude
where I set up camp long ago.
Up here in the polished ether,
untrampled and sparse, smooth as glass,
a hushed song closes in.

**Charles Augustus Smith**

It was way before
Emily Dickinson became my heroine
that I visited Charles Augustus Smith,
a painter in his 70s, brought by
a local gallery owner introducing me to art.
It was about 1978, more than thirty years
after he left his successful career
as an artist in advertising
and exhibiting painter in New York City.

This dramatic shift—withdrawing
from the established art world—
was caused by his reading
of Emily Dickinson's poetry.
From then on he painted only for himself.

A frail, bespectacled man of average height,
gentle in demeanor, he lived
in a small apartment of meager décor,
dirty walls badly in need of paint.
I never learned how he supported himself.

He painted landscapes—trees, forests—
and delicate floral arrangements in vases,
far into the night. His large rectangular
canvases were stacked against the walls.
Honest, alive, and a monument to his ethic,
his flowers danced. His textured
trees bristled.

His solitude, his presence for his process,
born of inner promptings, like
Emily Dickinson, called me back
to my beginnings. Yet I had to take
years of art classes and exhibit paintings,
before I could return to the same heartbeat
as Charles Augustus Smith and Emily Dickinson.

## Exhalation

When you are a skinny, anxious kid, growing up
in the Bronx, clothed in flouncy skirts by your mother
to hide your slight frame, and you love
drawing and painting,
you find yourself staring at art supplies
in the Arthur Brown & Company store window—
colored and graphite pencils, pastels, tubes of oil paint,
watercolors, and brushes in resplendent sets,
fanned out and framed by sketch pads and easels.
You buy coveted charcoal and pads with your allowance
at the art supply store under the Jerome Avenue El,
but don't know what to do with them. You receive
a Jon Gnagy Art Kit and follow his drawing lessons
on TV with satisfaction because you can copy well.
You buy oil paint and a canvas with your penny collection
at Macy's and make a small painting of a bird,
but you don't know anything about oil paint
and you are disappointed in your work. Your mother
enrolls you in a Saturday morning art class
at the Rhodes School in Manhattan, and your report card says
you have an excellent sense of color and composition,
good draftsmanship, but you don't think
well of your work. And you copy, copy, copy pictures
because you don't know what else to do. You don't draw
from visual memory like your friend who illustrates
the class newspapers, so, in the end,
your art amounts to nothing in your view

and you grow up and search for your own way,
read about Buddhist art and philosophy and wish
you had had a painter-scholar father who sat meditating
in his robes by your bedside as you fell asleep each night,

suffusing you with serenity, who taught you
to follow your breath, to follow *The Way*,
taught you to grind ink, dip your brush—
press, let up, press, curl—taught you to paint
organic lines shining on rice paper

and you learn to trust your intuition, you explore,
experiment, study art, and play, play, play.

**Mentor**
        for Marguerite Fuller

Her horses reared; their nostrils flared.
Carved out of clay or inked buoyantly on wet paper,
they crowded her studio—kitchen, living room,
dining room combined. Clay and tools sprawled
around her kitchen sink, printing press and drawing table
anchored her living room.
She received visitors upstairs in her bedroom.

A slim woman in black dress, graying hair—
practical shoes that squeaked across the hardwood floor,
she stared quizzically through rimless eyeglasses,
sailed her ship into the fray, like Samuel de Champlain
creating New France, took art to public school children,
to exhibits at the Somerstown Gallery.

She studied passersby from her window,
like Picasso studied African masks,
models for her figure drawings.
Occasionally she put her feet up,
read novels for three days.
She, supported by a trust,
could live like this, unlike my family,
immigrants grappling with survival.

She the older, single, independent artist—
I, the wife, mother, mannered, middle-aged seeker—
exploring new materials, new freedoms,
a change from practical pursuits,
taught by my assimilating family.

I plunged into clay, its cool wetness
sliding through my fingers,
fashioned a guy on a motorcycle,
drew in her ink-on-wet-paper technique,
shaping tomatoes that seeped and swirled,
forged etchings of trees and lilies.

Where did she come from?
I never did find out.
To whom did she belong?
All of us, I think.

## My Childhood Poet

When my mother read me poems
from *A Child's Garden of Verses*
they must have enchanted her
as much as they delighted me—
she who, on any ordinary day,
would suddenly burst out with a poem
or song learned in her childhood.
It must have been Stevenson's
child-like mind, his musicality,
rhyming, questions, and teasing
that appealed to us, lifted us up.
I loved his poems as much as I loved
to draw and paint.

II
At the Robert Louis Stevenson Cottage
in Saranac Lake, in this place he came
to cure his TB, I linger before
his childhood photos,
his yachting cap, ice skates,
smoking jacket, letters, a lock of his hair,
and then—
and then—
a glass case of woodblocks.
He carved woodblocks for his stepson
to print on his press
to illustrate *Moral Emblems*—
pirates and anglers, an elephant,
an eagle, a mill, a boat—
eighteen in all.
At the Stevenson Cottage in Saranac Lake
our hearts were joined as artists, too!

**An Unknown Woman**
      for Alice Koller

I was an unknown woman like her. We didn't know our truth—
what we felt, loved, lived for—couldn't name it, didn't know
how to find it. She was single, a doctor of philosophy.
I was married with two children, formerly
a kindergarten teacher and school psychologist.
She longed for a breath of mother love. She said,
*I don't live anywhere. I perch.* I longed for a prominent place
in a family whose hearts were captured by older male cousins.
I said, *I feel invisible.*

Tired of running after things that eluded her, she cut all ties—
rented a house on Nantucket, in Siasconset,
for three months in winter—five rooms overlooking the moors,
took long beach walks with Logos, her German Shepherd puppy,
asked herself endless questions, wrote in her journal—
slowly listed things she loved, slowly learned to make decisions
that suited *her*.

I found her book accidently at *Books N' Things*.
She taught me how to ask questions. I filled notebooks—
naming the colors of my fears, shame, resentments and grief,
claiming my kindness, compassion, curiosity, creativity,
and spiritual persuasions,
my work supporting children and families,
my fondness for folk dancing, folk songs, folk instruments—
expressions of the people.

In an extroverted world
I raised my hand as a solitude.

## Journal of a Solitude
### for May Sarton

In the photograph
she sits at her desk in a cheerful room—
  large windows,
  floor-to-ceiling bookcases,
  a fireplace,
  a comfy chair in the corner
in this room of her own,
in this house of her own.

I planned our vacation that year
  to the Monadnock Mountains,
  to Nelson, New Hampshire,
  to see her house.

She needed time
  to be,
  to meditate,
  mull over encounters,
  learn the meaning of her experiences,
  to make her darkness conscious,
  to take possession of herself.

After all, she was a writer
  compelled to write about her inward journey—
  to leave the door open for the holy,
  to write to the bone—transparent, naked,
  to perhaps bring some comfort to others.

She wrote...*open-ended time is the only luxury
that really counts,*
  even as she faced boredom, panic,
  and frustrating *errand time.*

And I, sitting in my recliner
      in my bedroom, next to my desk,
      bookcases in an adjacent room,
      paints and easel in the basement,
      read of her pursuits joyfully—
      —a map for a monk's life.

## For Stevie Smith

I remember Glenda Jackson playing *Stevie*,

> Stevie with Aunt, her *Lion Aunt,*
> a buxom, bold, straight talker,
> who helped to raise her—
> such sweet love—

she now taking care of Aunt,
in their little Victorian home in suburban Palmers Green
on Avondale Road.

Stevie wrote novels and poems about it—

> novels in an odd, original voice—
> absurd vignettes about everyday life,
> funny and intimate, with sketches and doodles—

> poems with playful rhyming meter,
> yet dark—deeply morbid, about loneliness and deat
> performed on the BBC.

I watched with fascination

> how Stevie renounced popularity,
> relished domestic life with Aunt—
> so deeply comfortable.

> She never married,
> said *romantic love* was missing in her,
> said she'd make a bad wife—
> too selfish, too interested in her own thoughts—

much preferred friendships—
lunch, dinner, art museums,
country weekends with literary friends
who loved her eccentric spirit.

So what if she lived an uncommon life?

> She was nervous, shy,
> sensitive, melancholy,
> chronically fatigued—
> not cut out for University life,
> not cut out for the business world,
> secretary to a publisher—an undemanding job.

Why was hers called a tragic life? It seemed so full and genuine—

> such a gift to me—
> a middle-aged woman,
> quiet, sensitive, artistic,

carving out my own reality.

**Emily and Me: A Sestina**

I met her on Broadway, *The Belle of Amherst*.
Right then she spoke about Self and choice.
Right then she spoke about introspection.
Right then I felt a surge of spirit.
Right then my soul heard its destiny—
a path of solitude and revelation.

She wasn't always fixed in a life of revelation.
She took part in society as a young girl in Amherst.
Only gradually did it appear, her cloistered destiny.
Only gradually did shyness seal her choice.
Only slowly did it rise in me, the voice of spirit.
Only slowly did I retreat into introspection.

She wrote to mentors with growing introspection.
She sent them slant rhymes and revelations.
Her father's books quenched her thirsty spirit,
in this patriarchal college town, this house in Amherst.
I wrote poems and essays—they were my choice,
strengthened by reading; this was my destiny.

Internal riches fed her destiny.
Perseverance fueled her introspection.
Questioning God was often her choice.
She addressed eternity in revelations
in her house, in nature—her gardens in Amherst.
And I found my truth in practices of the spirit.

Revivals and conversions were not of her spirit.
Immortality was her hoped for destiny.
In puritan New England, in the town of Amherst,
she left the church for a life of introspection.
I explored religions for personal revelation,
and left formal prayer. That was my choice.

She penned arcane poems, an internal choice.
Obscure images elated her spirit.
Abrupt rhythms aided her revelations.
Narrative poetry was my destiny,
finding insights in writing, in introspection.
Yes, I visited her home, her house in Amherst.

By choice I followed her. It was my destiny.
My spirit asked indulgence in introspection.
Revelation was my gift from the belle of Amherst.

www.ingramcontent.com/pod-product-compliance
Lightning Source LLC
LaVergne TN
LVHW041638060526
838200LV00040B/1625